The Oxford Picture Dictionary

for the

CONTENT AREAS

Dorothy Kauffman
Gary Apple

OXFORD
UNIVERSITY PRESS

Oxford University Press
198 Madison Avenue
New York, NY 10016 USA

Great Clarendon Street
Oxford OX2 6DP England

Oxford New York
Athens Auckland Bangkok Bogota Buenos Aires
Calcutta Cape Town Chennai Dar es Salaam Delhi
Florence Hong Kong Istanbul Karachi Kuala Lumpur
Madrid Melbourne Mexico City Mumbai Nairobi Paris
São Paulo Singapore Taipei Tokyo Toronto Warsaw

and associated companies in
Berlin Ibadan

OXFORD is a trademark of Oxford University Press.

ISBN 0-19-434338-3 (softcover)
ISBN 0-19-434336-7 (hardcover)

Library of Congress Cataloging-in-Publication Data
Kauffman, Dorothy
The Oxford picture dictionary for the content areas/Dorothy
Kauffman, Gary Apple.
        p. cm.
Summary: A vocabulary teaching tool designed for students
between third and fifth grades, with words drawn from the'
subjects of social studies, history, science, and math.
  ISBN 0-19-434338-3 (softcover). —ISBN 0-19-434336-7
(hardcover)
  1. Picture dictionaries, English—Juvenile literature.
[1. Vocabulary.] I. Apple, Gary. II. Title.
PE1629.K38   1999
423'.1—dc21   98-36196
                                               CIP
                                               AC

Editorial Manager: Shelagh Speers
Project Editor: Charles Flynn Hirsch
Associate Editor: Stephen McGroarty
Editorial Assistants: Francesca Merlini, Peter Graham
Senior Production Editor: Paul B. Phillips
Elementary Design Manager: Doris Chen Pinzon
Designer: Nona Reuter, John Daly
Art Buyers: Alex Rockafellar; Paula Radding, Bill SMITH Studios
Production Manager: Abram Hall

Cover design by Nona Reuter & Doris Chen Pinzon

Printing (last digit): 10 9 8 7 6 5 4 3 2 1

Printed in Singapore.

Illustrations by Wendy Wassink Ackison, Garin Baker,
Kim Barnes/Artworks New York, S. Talmond Brown,
Rob Burman, Dan Burr, Sal Catalano, Mary Chandler,
Mona Diane Conner, Dom D'Andrea, Grace DeVito, Jim Effler
c/o American Artists Rep. Inc., Russell Farrell c/o American
Artists Rep. Inc., Jeff Foster, Michael Garland, John Paul
Genzo, GeoSystems Global Corporation, David Henderson,
Aleta Jenks, Uldis Klavins, Jerry Lofaro c/o American Artists
Rep. Inc., Alan Male c/o American Artists Rep. Inc.,
Lee MacLeod, William Maughan, Tom Newsom, Larry Salk,
Bill Schmidt, Wendy Smith-Griswold, Tim Spransy,
Taylor Stamper, Shannon Stirnweis, Ron Tanovitz

Acknowledgements

The Publisher would like to thank the following people for their
editorial help and expertise: Charles Davis, Emilia Finan,
Debbie Lazarus, Rene Minkowitz, Lyn Perino, Elva Reynoso,
Zenaida Rosario, Susan Sernau, Margaret Simpson, Deborah
Supple, Nancy Ward

The Authors and Publisher would like to thank the following
people for their help in creating this book.

In California:
Doreen Aghajanian, Clarinda Aldrich, Virginia Amlie,
Anita Beeth, Manuel Bella, Susan Cleaver, Barbara Cohen,
Joe Cortez, Suzanne Crago-Schneider, Becky Cummins,
Denise Dacles, Mari Fedora, Sharon Futa, Elain Gordon,
Mary Gyselbrecht, Eric Hallman, Rose Mary Johnston,
Marilyn Van Leeuwens, Scott Love, Sharon Lyle,
Joan McCarthy, Pat Melville, Irma Parisi, Mandy Price,
Tracy Ramont, Chris Salcido, José Santiago, Janice Smalley,
Helen Soohoo, Judy Sullivan, Sarah Sullivan, Maxine Tanney,
Joan Tetreault, Sharon White, Eunice Wilson, Jim Zechmeister

In New Jersey:
Joan Bornheimer, Michelle Shields-Buono, Alexis J. Dougherty,
David Hewitt, Gary Kabbash, Alice Larkins, Susan Opper,
Mary Webb

In New York:
Nancy Claire, Evelyn Espino, Judy Geller-Marlowe,
Martin Howfield, Shirley Hunter, Virginia Jama, Carole Kaye,
Susan Litt, Susan Mayberger, Marina Moran, Dolly O'Neil-
Mejia, Carol Pertchik, Joan Ross-Keyes, Jane Sperling,
Barbara Wein, Phyllis Zieger

In Texas:
Gracie Alvear, Gloria Ayala, Marilyn Baker, Andrea Bermudez,
Mary Chapa, Crista Cloutier, Pat Collins, Debbie Coonrod,
Betty Lou Crowell, Dana Darden, Barbara Davis,
Geraldine Day, Yolanda Del Rio, Rosemary Denk,
Katrina Donahue, Aracely Gans, Mary Garces, Lois Gnade,
Jo Marie Greiser, Jane Gilhooley, Leticia Gomez,
Gaye Gustavson, Marybeth Jacobson, Natalie Kagan,
David Kelley, Cindy Kunkel, Hazel Lowrance, Blanca Martinez,
Suzie McNeese, Doris Morgan, Amy Pane, Roseanne Saul,
José Antonio Sepulveda, Susan Stevens, Linda Sullivan,
Ellie Torres, Oralia Villareal, Lynn Wong

For Bonnie and Amy, two superb educators who have
provided me with endless support and encouragement.
                                    —Gary

To my editors Shelagh Speers, Eileen Mahood-José, and
Charles Hirsch, thank you for your vision and guidance.
To my husband, Robert E. Kauffman, my guardian angel,
thank you for your unflagging confidence and love.
                                    —dotti

PREFACE

The Oxford Picture Dictionary for the Content Areas is designed for elementary school students who are learning English. The Dictionary presents over 1500 words drawn from the content areas of social studies, history, science, and math. The words are presented in full-page illustrations that place each word in context.

Dictionary Organization

- **Units and Topics.** The Dictionary is divided into eight thematic units. Each unit is divided into separate topics. The first unit relates to ESL students' experiences in their schools, families, and communities. The next seven units focus on the content areas of social studies, history, science, and math. Each topic has a full-page illustration which appears on the right-hand page. The left-hand page features the content words, each accompanied by a small picture to call out the word in the illustration. These "callouts" help students isolate each word as they search for it in the context of the illustration. Individual topics generally feature 12 to 20 callouts.

- **Appendix.** The appendix includes vocabulary and illustrations for numbers, time, money, colors, a calendar, food, clothing, and a map of the world.

- **Word List.** An index of words follows the appendix. The callout words appear in black. The key words that appear in a topic's title or within an illustration appear in pink.

Using the Dictionary as a Program

The Dictionary can be used by itself to supplement existing ESL programs, or it can be used with its additional components to make a suitable English language curriculum. These components include:

- *Teacher's Book*
- *Reproducibles Collection*
- *Workbook*
- *Cassettes*
- *Wall Charts*
- *Transparencies*

The *Reproducibles Collection* is a boxed set of four books:

- *Word and Picture Cards*
- *Worksheets*
- *Content Readings*
- *Content Chants*

The *Content Readings* explain the topics as they are depicted in the illustrations. *Content Chants* provide further practice in language and content. Readings of the *Dictionary, Content Readings,* and *Content Chants* are available on cassettes. The *Picture Dictionary* is available in both monolingual and bilingual editions.

TABLE OF CONTENTS

THE CLASSROOM

 1. student

 2. teacher

 3. desk

 4. chair

 5. table

 6. book

 7. computer

 8. pencil

 9. pen

 10. crayon

 11. paper

 12. notebook

 13. ruler

 14. chalkboard

 15. bulletin board

 16. map

 17. overhead projector

 18. pencil sharpener

 19. cassette player

 20. wastebasket

THE SCHOOL

 1. playground

 2. office

 3. principal

 4. secretary

 5. cafeteria

 6. gym

 7. coach

 8. hall

 9. water fountain

 10. locker

 11. boys room

 12. girls room

 13. custodian

 14. auditorium

 15. stairs

 16. library

 17. librarian

 18. media center

READ

THE HOUSE

 1. porch

 2. window

 3. door

 4. basement

 5. kitchen

 6. cupboard

 7. living room

 8. floor

 9. bathroom

 10. toilet

 11. sink

 12. bathtub

 13. shower

 14. bedroom

 15. closet

 16. wall

 17. ceiling

 18. attic

 19. roof

 20. chimney

THE FAMILY

 1. grandparents

 7. baby

 2. grandmother

 8. sister

 3. grandfather

 9. brother

 4. parents

 10. aunt

 5. mother

 11. uncle

 6. father

 12. cousins

THE CITY

1. restaurant

2. newsstand

3. hotel

4. post office

5. department store

6. office building

7. apartment building

8. church

9. mosque

10. temple

11. parking garage

12. bank

13. movie theater

14. police station

15. subway

16. bus

17. taxi

18. garbage truck

19. helicopter

20. traffic light

THE SUBURBS

 1. street

 2. sidewalk

 3. crosswalk

 4. corner

 5. block

 6. stop sign

7. mailbox

8. fire hydrant

9. yard

 10. garden

 11. garage

 12. driveway

 13. park

 14. swimming pool

 15. gas station

 16. van

 17. car

 18. motorcycle

 19. bicycle

 20. basketball

THE COUNTRY

 1. farm

 2. barn

 3. silo

 4. path

 5. fence

 6. chicken coop

 7. orchard

 8. pasture

 9. pond

 10. woods

 11. hills

 12. field

 13. road

 14. stream

 15. bridge

 16. airplane

 17. train

 18. truck

 19. tractor

 20. wagon

THE HOSPITAL

 1. patient

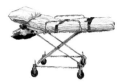 10. crutches

 2. doctor

 11. cast

 3. examination table

 12. wheelchair

 4. bandage

 13. bed

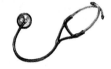 5. stethoscope

 14. pillow

 6. thermometer

 15. blanket

 7. medicine

 16. ambulance

 8. X ray

 17. paramedic

 9. nurse

 18. stretcher

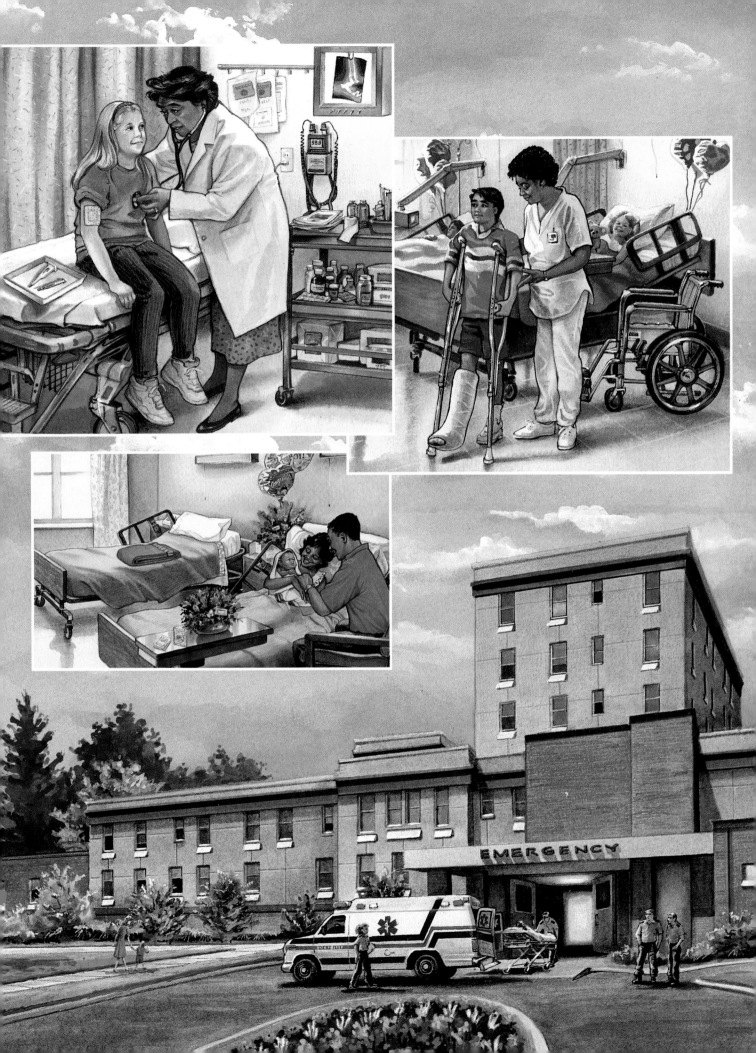

PEOPLE AT WORK

 1. construction worker

 2. electrician

 3. carpenter

 4. mail carrier

 5. firefighter

 6. police officer

 7. mechanic

 8. messenger

 9. musician

 10. painter

 11. computer operator

 12. writer

 13. dentist

 14. dental assistant

 15. hairdresser

 16. plumber

 17. pharmacist

 18. salesperson

FIRE STATION Nº 67

THE UNITED STATES

AL	Alabama	IN	Indiana	NV	Nevada	TN	Tennessee
AK	Alaska	IA	Iowa	NH	New Hampshire	TX	Texas
AZ	Arizona	KS	Kansas	NJ	New Jersey	UT	Utah
AR	Arkansas	KY	Kentucky	NM	New Mexico	VT	Vermont
CA	California	LA	Louisiana	NY	New York	VA	Virginia
CO	Colorado	ME	Maine	NC	North Carolina	WA	Washington
CT	Connecticut	MD	Maryland	ND	North Dakota	WV	West Virginia
DE	Delaware	MA	Massachusetts	OH	Ohio	WI	Wisconsin
DC	District of Columbia	MI	Michigan	OK	Oklahoma	WY	Wyoming
FL	Florida	MN	Minnesota	OR	Oregon	GU	Guam
GA	Georgia	MS	Mississippi	PA	Pennsylvania	AS	American Samoa
HI	Hawaii	MO	Missouri	RI	Rhode Island	VI	U.S. Virgin Islands
ID	Idaho	MT	Montana	SC	South Carolina	PR	Puerto Rico
IL	Illinois	NE	Nebraska	SD	South Dakota		

The United States

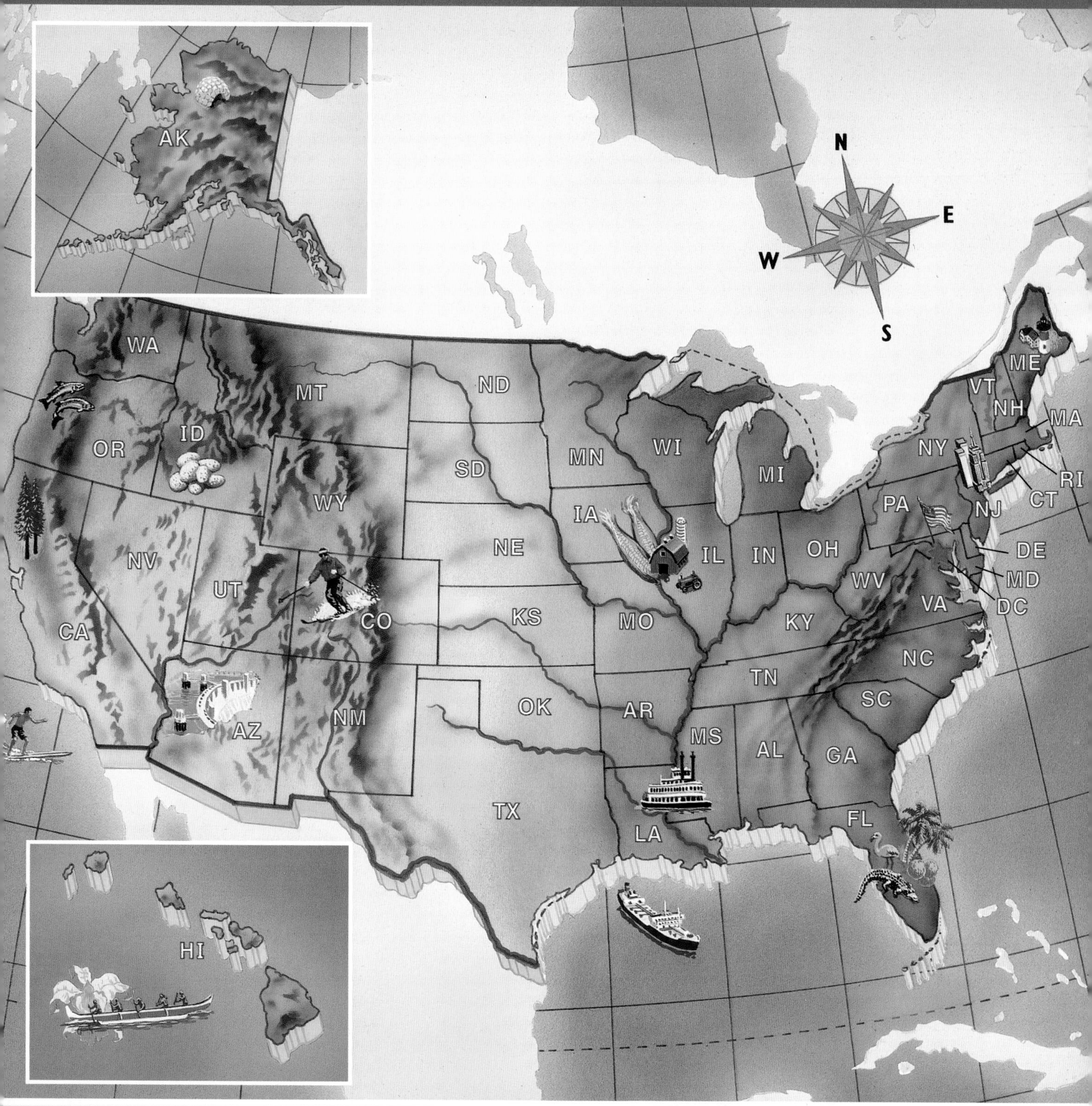

N
E
W
S

AK

WA
MT
ND
ME
VT
NH
MA
OR
ID
WY
SD
MN
WI
MI
NY
RI
CT
NV
UT
NE
IA
IL
IN
OH
PA
NJ
DE
MD
DC
CA
CO
KS
MO
KY
WV
VA
AZ
NM
OK
AR
TN
NC
SC
TX
MS
AL
GA
LA
FL

HI

U.S. Territories

GU

AS

VI

PR

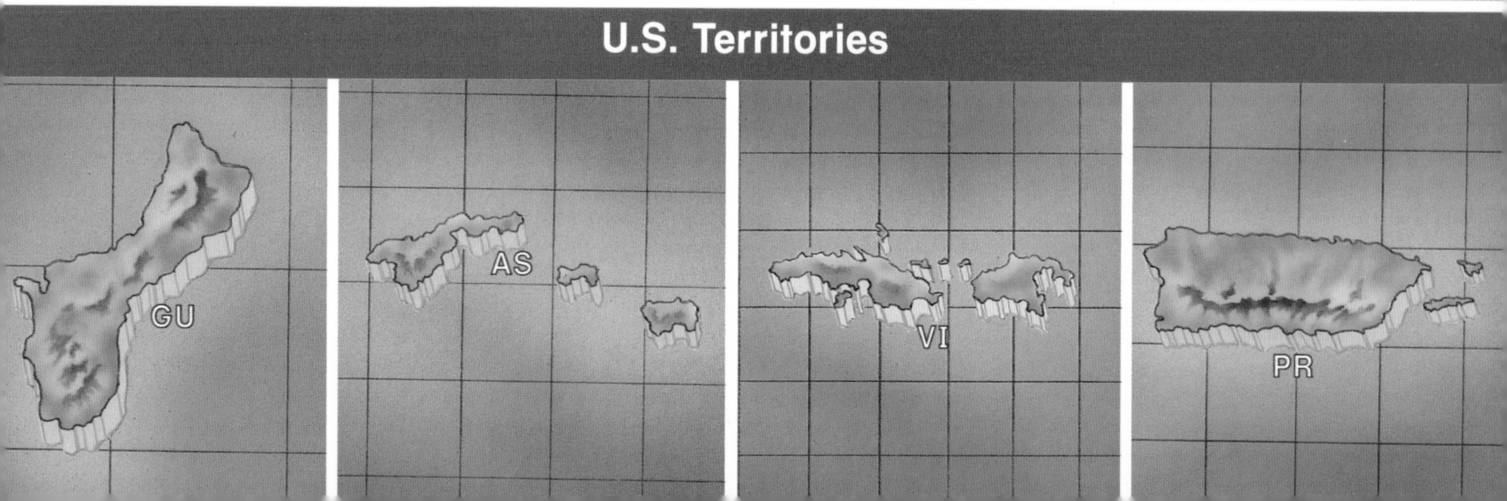

THE NORTHEAST
Communication and Finance

 1. stock market

 2. stocks and bonds

 3. businessperson

 4. newspaper

 5. magazine

 6. buy

 7. sell

 8. headline

 9. advertisement

 10. studio

 11. newscaster

 12. television

 13. radio

 14. telephone

 15. satellite

 16. Statue of Liberty

17. Liberty Bell

 18. The White House

GREETINGS FROM THE NORTHEAST!

THE SOUTH
Food Processing and Manufacturing

 1. sugarcane

 2. cotton

 3. rice

 4. crop

 5. sugar

 6. factory

 7. worker

 8. assembly line

 9. lumber

 10. cloth

 11. thread

 12. furniture

 13. raw materials

 14. goods

 15. port

 16. plantation

 17. Mississippi River

 18. Kennedy Space Center

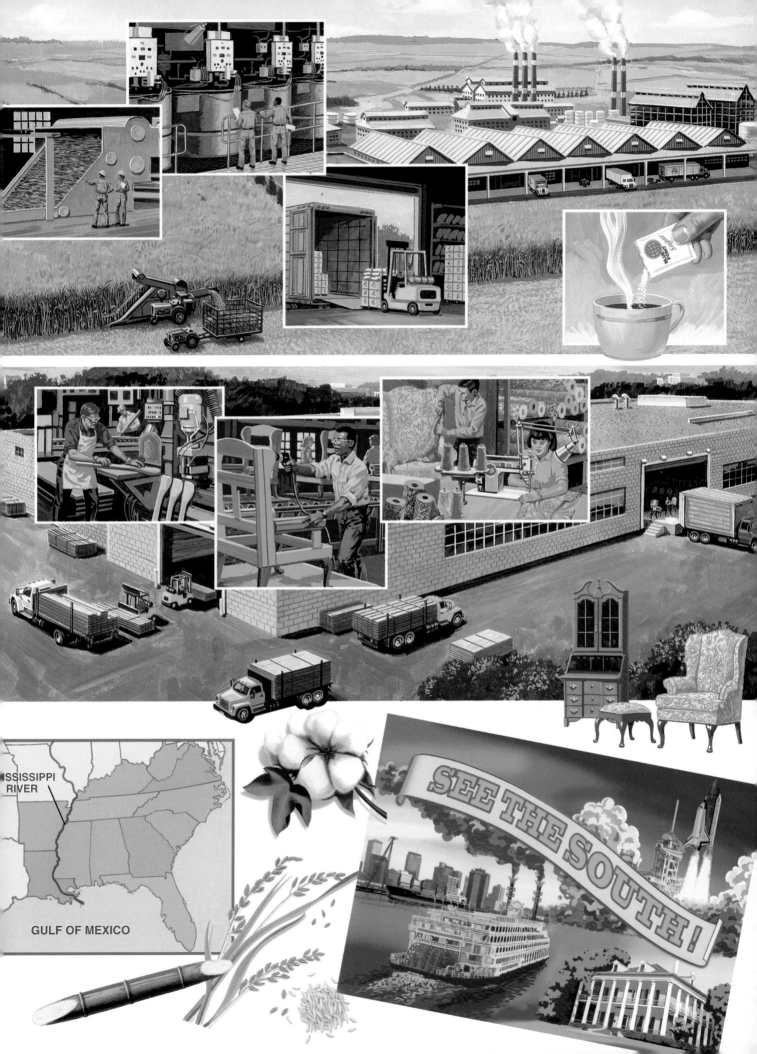

SSISSIPPI
RIVER

GULF OF MEXICO

SEE THE SOUTH!

THE MIDWEST
Agriculture and Dairy Farming

 1. dairy barn

 2. cattle

 3. farmhouse

 4. plant

 5. harvest

 6. plow

 7. combine

 8. hay

 9. wheat

 10. soybeans

 11. corn

 12. grain

 13. grain elevator

 14. Great Lakes

 15. Great Plains

 16. Mount Rushmore

COME TO THE MIDWEST!

THE WEST
Mining and Ranching

 1. open pit

 2. mine

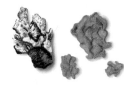 3. ore

 4. minerals

 5. ranch

 6. livestock

 7. corral

 8. cowgirl

 9. cowboy

 10. buffalo

 11. herd

 12. graze

 13. Rocky Mountains

 14. peak

 15. Continental Divide

 16. rodeo

 17. Yellowstone National Park

 18. Old Faithful

CONTINENTAL DIVIDE

YELLOWSTONE
NATIONAL
PARK

AROUND THE ROCKIES!

ZZ RANCH

THE NORTHWEST
Forestry and Fishing

 1. forest

 2. logging

 3. lumberjack

 4. chain saw

 5. redwood

 6. pine

 7. timber

 8. sawmill

 9. wood

 10. sawdust

 11. fish

 12. cannery

 13. boat

 14. net

 15. rainfall

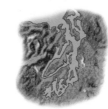 16. Puget Sound

 17. Space Needle

 18. Alaska Pipeline

VISIT THE NORTHWEST!

THE SOUTHWEST
Managing Natural Resources

 1. well

 2. oil

 3. natural gas

 4. drill

 5. refinery

 6. pipeline

 7. tank

 8. gasoline

 9. water storage

 10. dam

 11. reservoir

 12. irrigation canal

 13. hydroelectric plant

 14. electricity

 15. Grand Canyon

 16. cactus

CALIFORNIA
US
66

THE BEAUTIFUL SOUTHWEST!

Hiking Trails

Flora & Fa

Piñon pine

Yucca turkeys

THE WEST COAST AND PACIFIC
Technology, Tourism, and Entertainment

 1. filmmaking

 2. actor

 3. actress

 4. director

 5. script

 6. camera

 7. set

 8. fiber optics

 9. laser

 10. microchip

 11. resort

 12. tourist

 13. surfing

 14. freeway

 15. shopping mall

 16. Golden Gate Bridge

THE TERRIFIC PACIFIC !

CANADA AND MEXICO

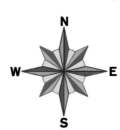 1. compass rose

 7. state

 2. legend

 8. capital

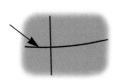 3. latitude

 9. money

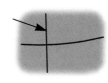 4. longitude

 10. totem pole

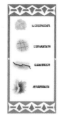 5. national border

 11. pyramid

 6. province

 12. silver

Canada

N
E
W
S

20
20

MacKenzie

Rocky Mountains

Fraser

St. Lawrence

Ottawa

Land
Ocean
Border
Mountain

Mexico

N
W
E
S

Rio Grande

Sierra Madres

10
diez pesos
10

Mexico City

THE NATIVE AMERICANS

 1. ceremony

 11. pictograph

 2. mask

 12. loom

 3. tepee

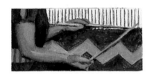 13. weave

TOPIC 19

 4. chief

 14. pottery

 5. tribe

 15. longhouse

 6. bow

 16. hunt

 7. arrow

 17. gather

 8. spear

 18. grind

 9. hide

 19. basket

 10. cliff dwelling

 20. wampum

EXPLORATION AND DISCOVERY

 1. route

 2. Vikings

 3. Leif Eriksson

 4. mast

 5. rope

6. knot

 7 cargo

 8. crew

 9. oar

 10. sailor

 11. prow

 12. wave

 13. Christopher Columbus

 14. Niña

15. Pinta

 16. Santa Maria

 17. sail

 18. jewelry

 19. native

 20. Ponce de León

Leif Eriksson

Ponce de León

Christopher Columbus

THE SPANISH MISSIONS

 1. pueblo

 2. fort

 3. trading post

 4. adobe

 5. gate

 6. arch

 7. patio

 8. fountain

 9. cross

 10. bell

 11. candles

 12. missionary

 13. teach

 14. Spanish soldiers

 15. ride

 16. sword

TOPIC
21

San Francisco

Tucson

Santa Fe

St. Augustine

San Diego

San Antonio

COLONIAL LIFE

TOPIC
22

 1. Pilgrims

 2. Thanksgiving

 3. town meeting

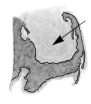 4. shore

 5. bay

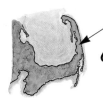 6. cape

 7. harbor

 8. common

 9. stockade

 10. meetinghouse

 11. courthouse

 12. inn

 13. mill

 14. blacksmith

 15. apprentice

 16. tobacco

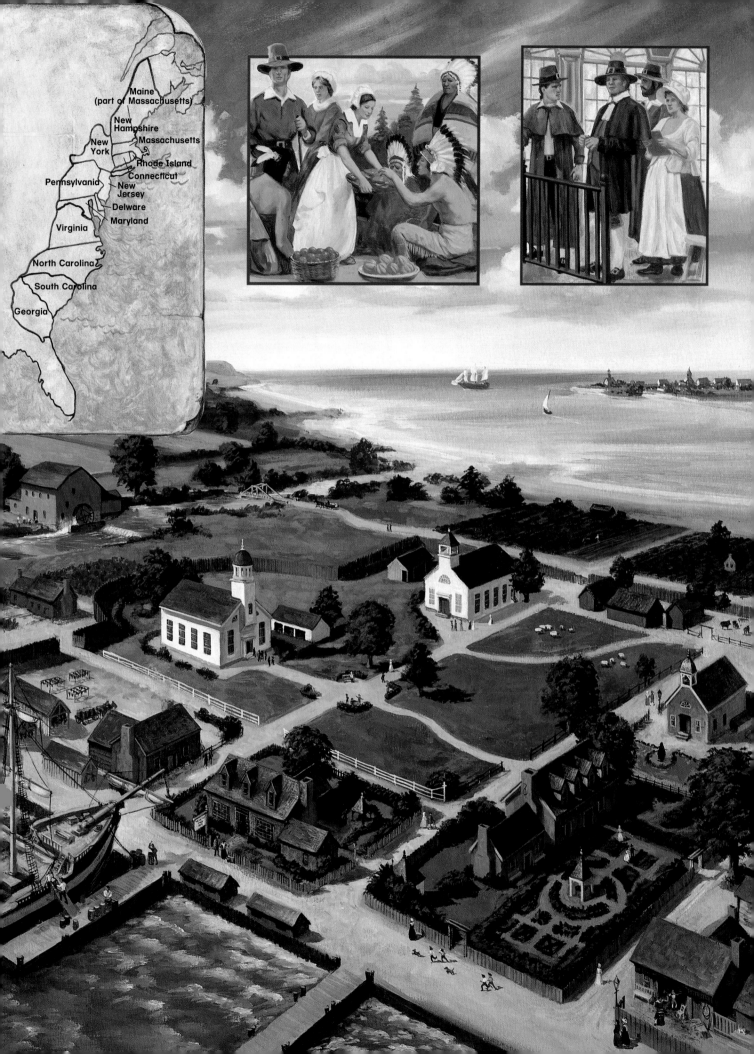

Maine
(part of Massachusetts)
New
Hampshire
New
York
Massachusetts
Rhode Island
Connecticut
Pennsylvania
New
Jersey
Delware
Maryland
Virginia
North Carolina
South Carolina
Georgia

THE REVOLUTIONARY WAR

 1. tea

 2. crate

 3. disguise

 4. tomahawk

 5. Paul Revere

 6. Old North Church

 7. steeple

 8. lantern

 9. sky

 10. battle

 11. redcoat

 12. Continental soldier

 13. minutemen

 14. rifle

 15. bayonet

 16. musket

 17. cannon

 18. cannonball

 19. powder horn

 20. load

THE BOSTON TEA PARTY

PAUL REVERE'S RIDE

THE BATTLE OF BUNKER HILL.

A NATION IS BORN

 1. Declaration of Independence

 9. write

 2. founding fathers

 10. quill

TOPIC 24

 3. printing press

 11. signature

 4. printer

 12. Thomas Jefferson

 5. pamphlet

 13. John Adams

 6. draw

 14. John Hancock

 7. cartoon

 15. King George III

 8. Benjamin Franklin

 16. Independence Hall

WESTWARD EXPANSION

 1. flatboat

 2. steamboat

 3. raft

 4. canoe

 5. canal

 6. pioneer

 7. wagon train

 8. covered wagon

 9. oxen

10. pass

 11. trail

 12. supplies

 13. barrel

 14. journal

 15. homestead

 16. cabin

 17. stagecoach

 18. campsite

 19. trapper

 20. pelt

1853 1803 1770

Westward Expansion

THE GOLD RUSH

 1. gold

 2. Sutter's Mill

 3. prospector

 4. pan

 5. dig

 6. dirt

 7. shovel

 8. pick

 9. tent

 10. hammer

 11. nail

 12. Levi Strauss

 13. mule

 14. clipper ship

 15. across

 16. around

THE CIVIL WAR

 1. Union

 2. Yankee

 3. Confederacy

 4. Rebel

 5. Abraham Lincoln

 6. Emancipation
Proclamation

 7. slave

 8. flag

 9. knapsack

 10. canteen

 11. ammunition

 12. uniform

 13. cemetery

 14. surrender

 15. Ulysses S. Grant

 16. Robert E. Lee

BULL RUN 1861

GETTYSBURG 1863

APPOMATTOX 1865

U.S. GOVERNMENT

 1. Constitution

 9. Oval Office

 2. Bill of Rights

 10. Great Seal

 3. citizens

 11. legislative branch

 4. candidate

 12. Senate

 5. vote

 13. House of Representatives

 6. ballot

 14. Congress

 7. executive branch

 15. judicial branch

 8. President

 16. Supreme Court

PEOPLE IN U.S. HISTORY

 1. Pocahontas
1595–1617

 2. George Washington
1731–1799

 3. Sequoya
1760–1843

 4. Sacajawea
1787–1812

 5. Frederick Douglass
1817–1895

 6. Harriet Tubman
1820–1913

 7. Clara Barton
1821–1912

 8. Thomas Edison
1847–1931

 9. Alexander Graham Bell
1847–1922

 10. Susan B. Anthony
1820–1906

 11. Henry Ford
1863–1947

 12. Helen Keller
1880–1968

 13. Eleanor Roosevelt
1884–1962

 14. Margaret Mead
1901–1978

 15. Cesar Chavez
1927–1993

 16. Martin Luther King, Jr.
1929–1968

TOPIC
29

PARTS OF THE BODY

 1. head

 2. hair

 3. eye

 4. ear

 5. nose

 6. mouth

 7. teeth

 8. chin

 9. neck

 10. shoulder

 11. arm

 12. elbow

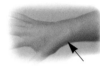 13. wrist

 14. hand

 15. finger

 16. thumb

 17. chest

 18. leg

 19. knee

 20. ankle

 21. foot

 22. toe

INSIDE THE HUMAN BODY

 1. skeleton

 2. bone

 3. skull

 4. jaw

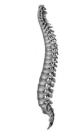 5. spine

 6. muscle

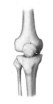 7. joint

 8. cartilage

 9. ligament

 10. tendon

 11. brain

 12. nerve

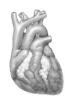 13. heart

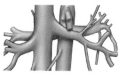 14. blood vessels

 15. artery

 16. vein

 17. lungs

 8. esophagus

 19. stomach

 20. intestine

TOPIC
31

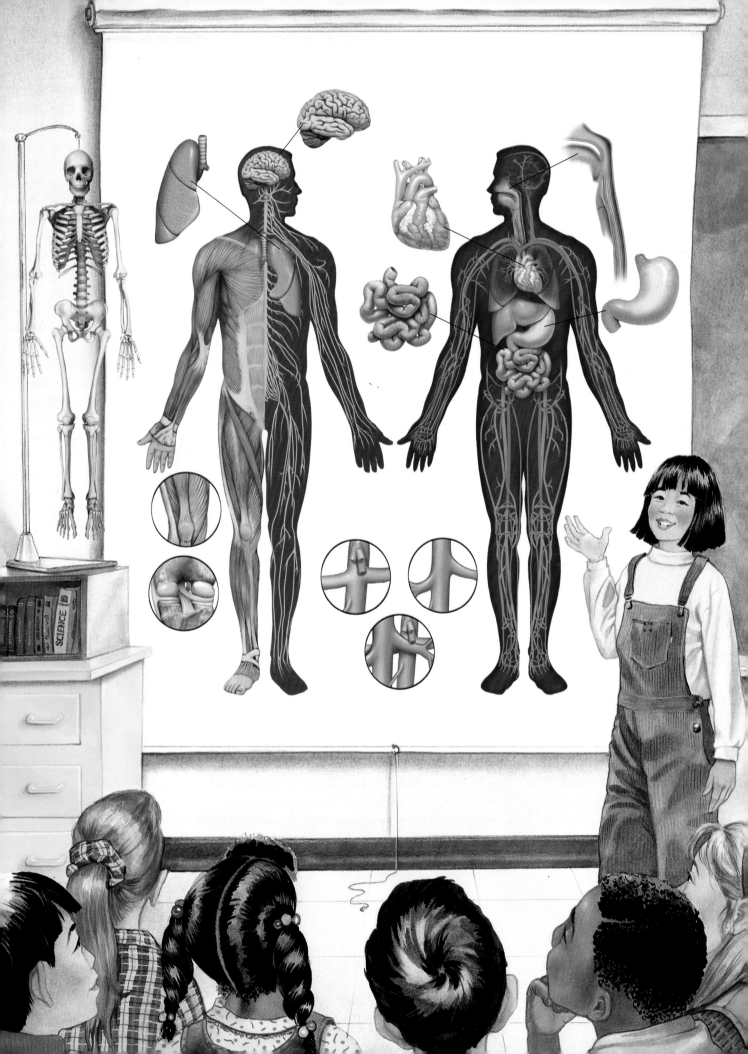

THE SENSES

 1. see

 2. bright

 3. dark

 4. hear

 5. loud

 6. soft

 7. smell

 8. fragrant

 9. foul

 10. taste

 11. sweet

 12. sour

 13. salty

 14. touch

 15. smooth

 16. rough

UNIT 4 THE HUMAN BODY

FEELINGS

 1. sick

 2. tired

 3. thirsty

 4. hot

 5. cold

 6. hungry

 7. silly

 8. shy

 9. scared

 10. surprised

 11. proud

 12. sad

 13. happy

 14. lonely

 15. excited

 16. angry

TOPIC 33

EXPLORING SCIENCE

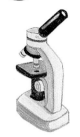 1. hand lens

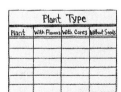 2. microscope

 3. tweezers

 4. slide

 5. cover glass

 6. chart

 7. data

 8. collection

 9. eyedropper

 10. fire extinguisher

 11. first aid kit

 12. safety glasses

 13. equipment

 14. model

 15. diagram

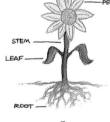 16. exhibit

Plan

Observe

Classify

Measure

Experiment

Report

LIVING ORGANISMS

 1. plants

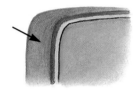 2. cells

 3. cell wall

 4. cell membrane

 5. nucleus

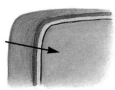 6. chromosome

7. cytoplasm

 8. photosynthesis

 9. monerans

 10. protists

 11. fungi

 12. animals

 13. vertebrates

14. invertebrates

TOPIC 35

Plants

Photosynthesis

Monerans

Protists

Fungi

Animals

PLANTS

 1. nut

 2. seed

 3. tree

 4. trunk

 5. limb

 6. bark

 7. leaf

 8. stem

 9. branch

 10. needle

 11. pinecone

 12. flower

 13. petal

 14. stamen

 15. pistil

 16. pollen

 17. bud

 18. stalk

 19. bulb

 20. root

VEGETABLES

 1. lettuce

 2. celery

 3. cabbage

 4. broccoli

 5. cauliflower

 6. carrot

 7. onion

 8. radish

 9. peppers

 10. lima beans

 11. cucumber

 12. string bean

 13. potato

 14. yam

 15. mushroom

 16. peas

TOPIC
37

FRUIT

 1. banana

 2. pineapple

 3. cantaloupe

 4. watermelon

 5. tomato

 6. peach

 7. cherry

 8. avocado

 9. pit

 10. apple

 11. pear

 12. citrus

 13. lemon

 14. lime

 15. orange

 16. grapefruit

 17. section

 18. rind

 19. strawberry

20. raspberry

TOPIC 38

SIMPLE ORGANISMS

 1. amoeba

 2. paramecium

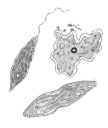 3. protozoans

4. flatworm

 5. roundworm

 6. segmented worms

 7. earthworm

 8. leech

 9. jellyfish

 10. coral

 11. starfish

 12. sponge

 13. sand dollar

 14. sea urchin

TOPIC 39

Single-Celled Organisms

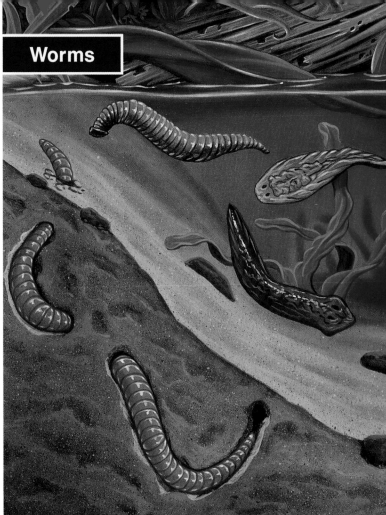

Worms

Sea Creatures

MOLLUSKS AND CRUSTACEANS

 1. octopus

 2. squid

 3. tentacles

 4. sea slug

 5. shells

 6. scallop

 7. clam

 8. oyster

 9. mussel

 10. conch

 11. snail

 12. lobster

 13. shrimp

 14. crab

 15. claw

 16. antennae

 17. barnacles

 18. crayfish

Mollusks

Crustaceans

INSECTS AND ARACHNIDS

 1. caterpillar

 2. chrysalis

 3. butterfly

 4. metamorphosis

 5. hive

 6. bee

 7. ladybug

 8. grasshopper

 9. cricket

 10. fly

 11. firefly

 12. mosquito

 13. ant

 14. thorax

 15. abdomen

 16. cockroach

 17. spider

 18. web

 19. tick

 20. scorpion

Insects

Arachnids

FISH

 1. bluefish

 2. swordfish

 3. shark

 4. tuna

 5. salmon

 6. pipefish

 7. eel

 8. cod

 9. sea horse

 10. fin

 11. gills

 12. scales

 13. bass

 14. minnow

 15. trout

 16. perch

 17. catfish

 18. goldfish

TOPIC 42

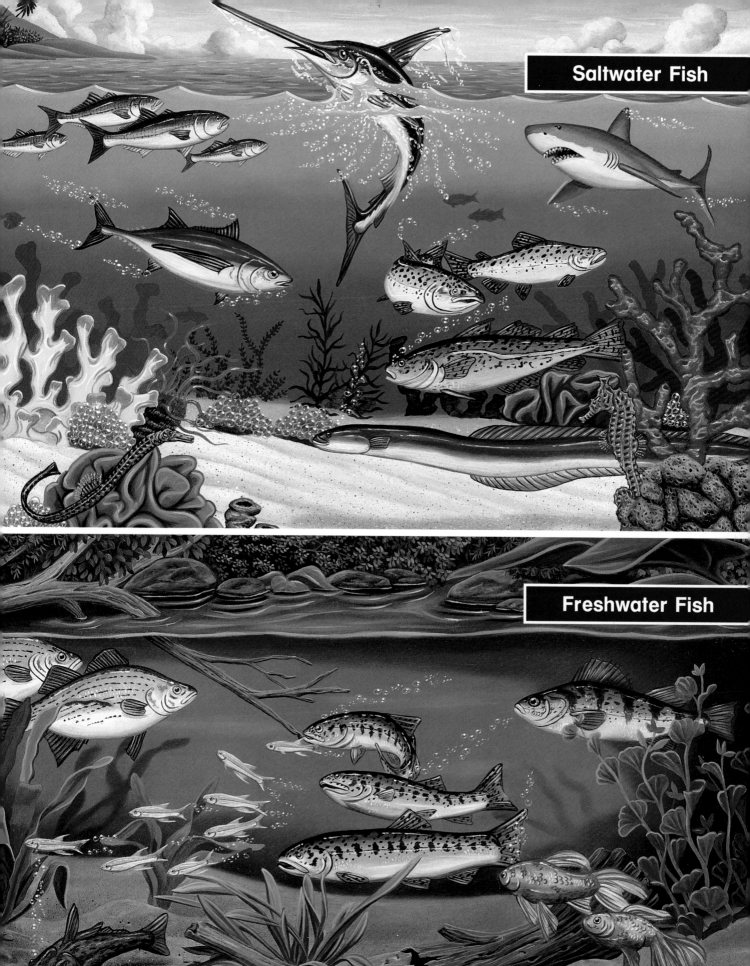

Freshwater Fish

AMPHIBIANS AND REPTILES

 1. salamander

 2. tail

 3. frog

 4. webbed foot

 5. tadpole

 6. toad

 7. alligator

 8. crocodile

 9. garter snake

 10. turtle

 11. chameleon

 12. iguana

 13. rattlesnake

 14. cobra

TOPIC 43

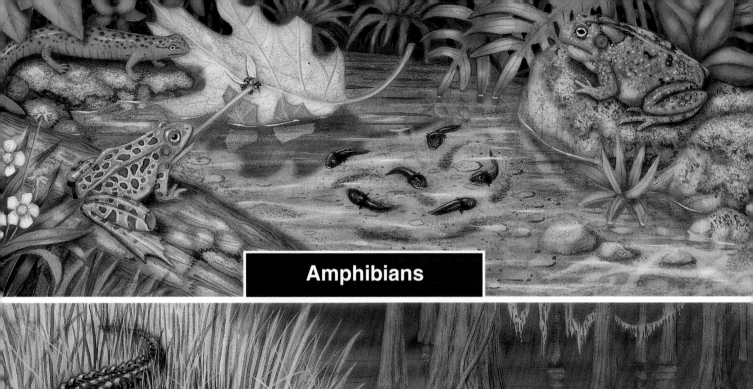

Amphibians

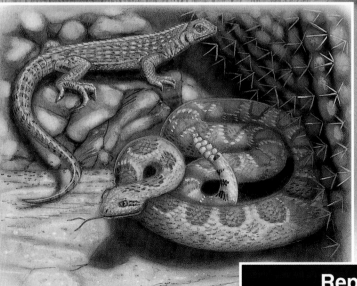

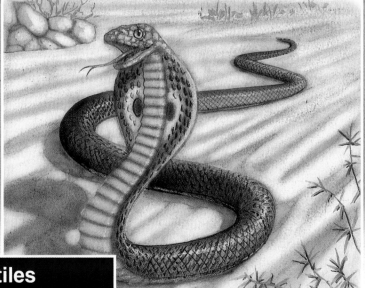

Reptiles

BIRDS

 1. pigeon

 2. sparrow

 3. robin

 4. cardinal

 5. goose

 6. duck

 7. hummingbird

 8. crow

 9. chicken

 10. turkey

 11. seagull

 12. eagle

 13. nest

 14. penguin

 15. ostrich

 16. peacock

 17. parrot

 18. beak

 19. feather

 20. wing

TOPIC 44

DOMESTIC MAMMALS

 1. goat

 2. kid

 3. sheep

 4. lamb

 5. rabbit

 6. bunny

 7. dog

 8. puppy

 9. cow

 10. calf

 11. cat

 12. kitten

 13. paw

 14. pig

 15. piglet

 16. horse

 17. foal

 18. forelegs

 19. hind legs

 20. hoof

TOPIC 45

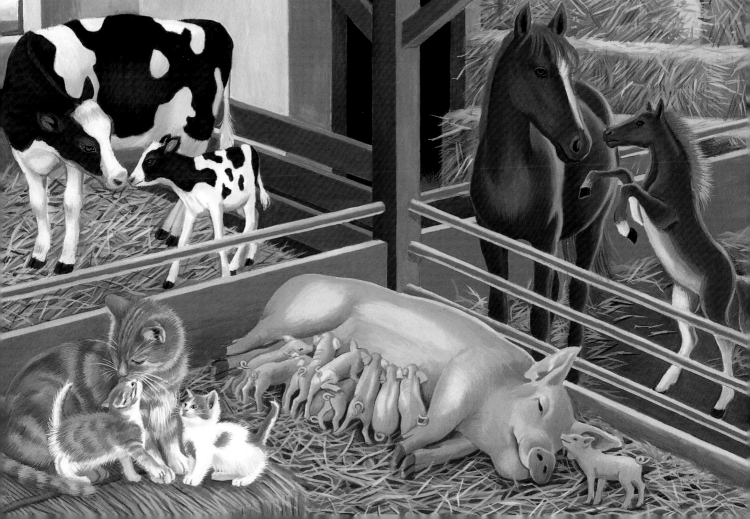

WILD MAMMALS

 1. squirrel

 2. bat

 3. opossum

 4. bear

 5. deer

6. fur

 7. whale

 8. dolphin

 9. camel

 10. kangaroo

 11. pouch

 12. tiger

 13. monkey

 14. giraffe

 15. lion

 16. zebra

 17. elephant

 18. tusk

TOPIC 46

PREHISTORIC ANIMALS

 1. dinosaurs

 2. triceratops

 3. ankylosaurus

 4. apatosaurus

 5. anatosaurus

 6. diplodocus

 7. dryosaurus

 8. brachiosaurus

 9. stegosaurus

 10. spike

 11. tyrannosaurus

 12. pteranodon

 13. allosaurus

 14. smilodon

 15. saber tooth

 16. fossil

TOPIC
47

Herbivores

Carnivores

OUR ENVIRONMENT
Problems and Solutions

 1. water pollution

 2. air pollution

 3. soil pollution

 4. smog

 5. smoke

 6. smokestack

 7. exhaust

 8. oil slick

 9. litter

 10. garbage

 11. can

 12. bottle

 13. landfill

 14. glass

 15. plastic

 16. metal

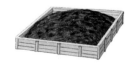 17. compost

 18. carpool

TOPIC **48**

REDUCE!
REUSE!
RECYCLE!

MATTER

 1. elements

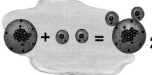 2. compound

 3. atom

 4. molecule

 5. proton

 6. neutron

 7. electron

 8. solid

 9. liquid

 10. gas

 11. physical change

 12. chemical change

 13. boil

 14. freeze

 15. melt

 16. evaporate

TOPIC
49

ENERGY AND MOTION

 1. simple machines

 2. axle

 3. pulley

 4. wheel

 5. wedge

6. inclined plane

 7. lever

 8. screw

 9. magnet

 10. gears

 11. push

 12. pull

 13. speed

 14. forces

 15. friction

 16. heat

 17. light

 18. sound

TOPIC 50

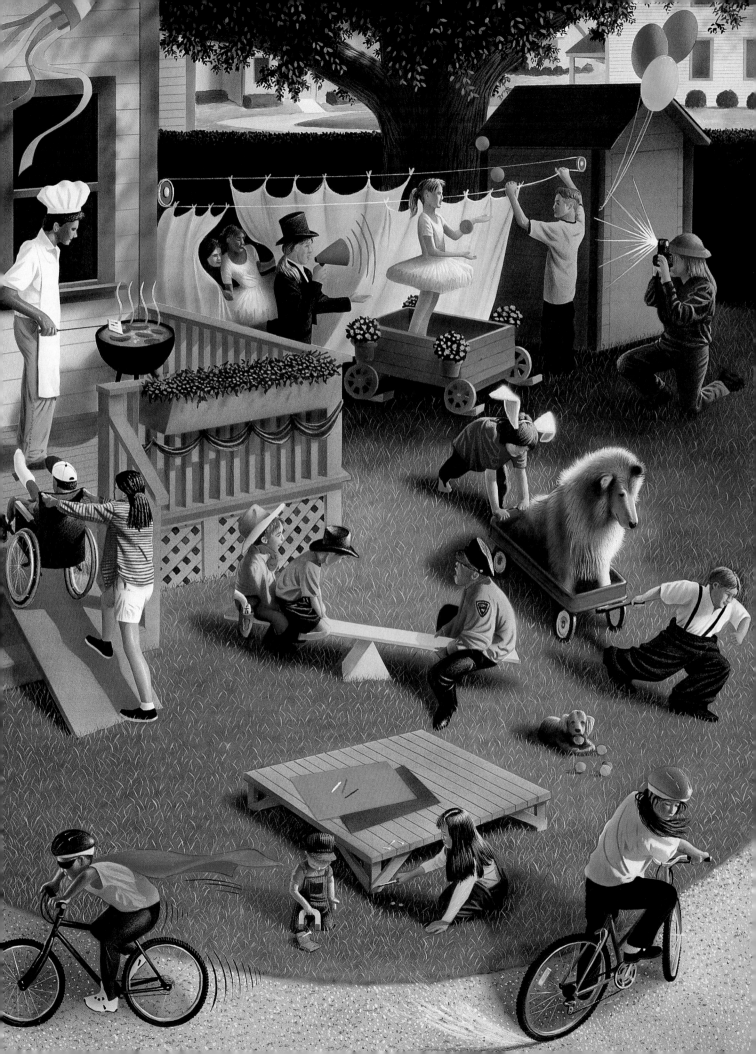

THE UNIVERSE

 1. solar system

 2. planets

 3. Sun

 4. Moon

 5. Mercury

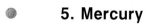 6. Venus

 7. Earth

 8. Mars

 9. Jupiter

 10. Saturn

 11. Uranus

 12. Neptune

13. Pluto

 14. star

 15. constellation

 16. meteor

 17. comet

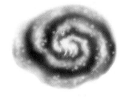 18. galaxy

TOPIC
51

THE EARTH AND ITS LANDFORMS

 1. mountain

 2. volcano

 3. lava

 4. plateau

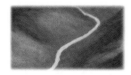 5. glacier

 6. valley

 7. river

 8. gulf

 9. ocean

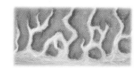 10. wetland

 11. peninsula

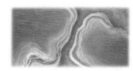 12. isthmus

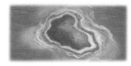 13. island

 14. layers

 15. crust

 16. mantle

 17. outer core

 18. inner core

CLIMATES AND LAND BIOMES

 1. temperate forest

 2. deciduous tree

 3. taiga

 4. evergreen tree

 5. tundra

 6. moss

 7. lichen

 8. tropical rain forest

 9. vines

 10. grassland

 11. grass

 12. desert

 13. sand

 14. polar zones

 15. temperate zones

 16. tropical zone

TOPIC
53

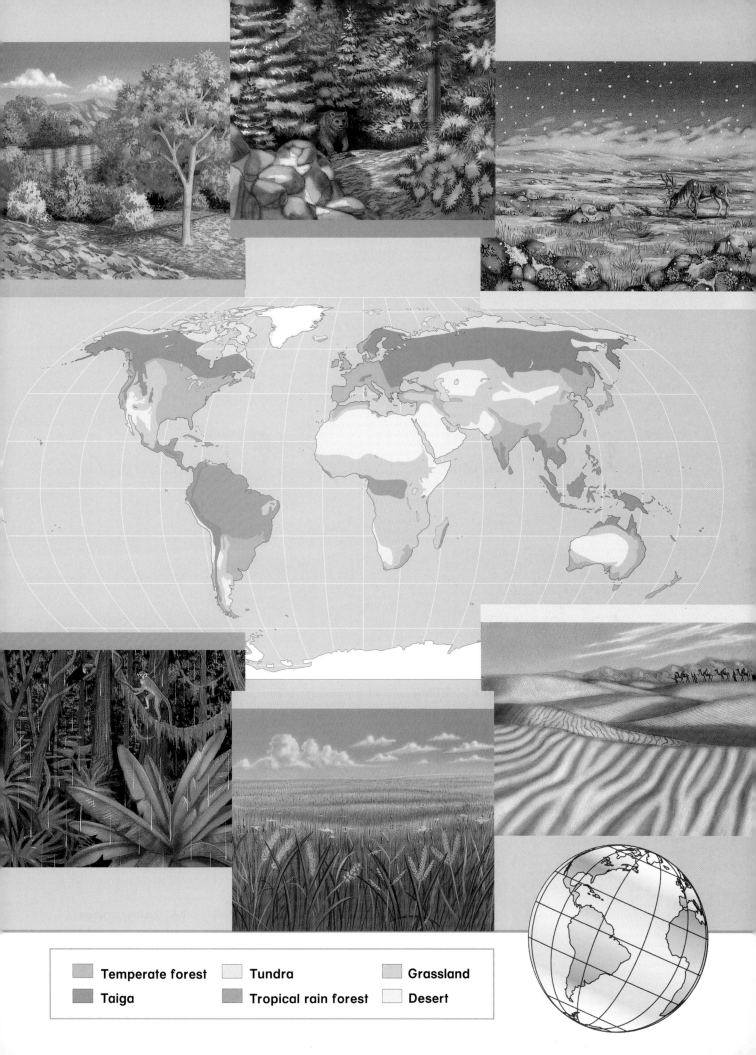

Temperate forest   Tundra   Grassland

Taiga   Tropical rain forest   Desert

WEATHER

 1. forecaster

 9. temperature

 2. sunshine

 10. storms

 3. snow

 11. blizzard

 4. wind

 12. hurricane

 5. cloud

 13. fog

 6. lightning

 14. tornado

 7. rain

 15. sleet

 8. rainbow

 16. atmosphere

TOPIC 54

EXPLORING MATH

 1. number line

X 9. multiply

0123456789 2. digits

$4 \times 3 = 12$ 10. product

 3. even numbers

÷ 11. divide

1 3 5 4. odd numbers

$6 \div 3 = 2$ 12. quotient

+ 5. add

> < = 13. comparisons

$4 + 1 = 5$ 6. sum

1 14. whole number

▬ 7. subtract

$\frac{1}{2}$ 15. fraction

$7 - 3 = 4$ 8. difference

$1\frac{1}{2}$ 16. mixed number

TOPIC 55

GEOMETRY I

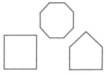 1. plane figures

 2. square

 3. rectangle

 4. triangle

 5. circle

 6. pentagon

 7. octagon

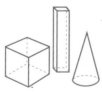 8. solid figures

 9. cube

 10. sphere

 11. cylinder

 12. cone

 13. rectangular prism

 14. lines

 15. line segment

 16. parallel

 17. perpendicular

 18. ray

GEOMETRY II

1. compass

2. circumference

3. diameter

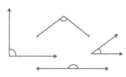
4. angles

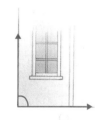
5. right angle

6. acute angle

7. obtuse angle

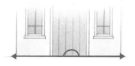
8. straight angle

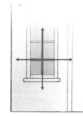
9. intersecting lines

10. perimeter

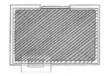
11. area

12. height

13. length

14. width

15. base

16. edge

17. symmetrical

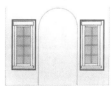
18. congruent figures

MEASUREMENT

 1. centimeter

 2. meter

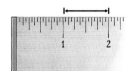 3. inch

 4. foot

 5. weight

 6. gram

 7. kilogram

 8. ounce

 9. pound

 10. ton

 11. mile

 12. teaspoon

 13. tablespoon

 14. cup

 15. liter

 16. pint

 17. quart

 18. gallon

TOPIC
58

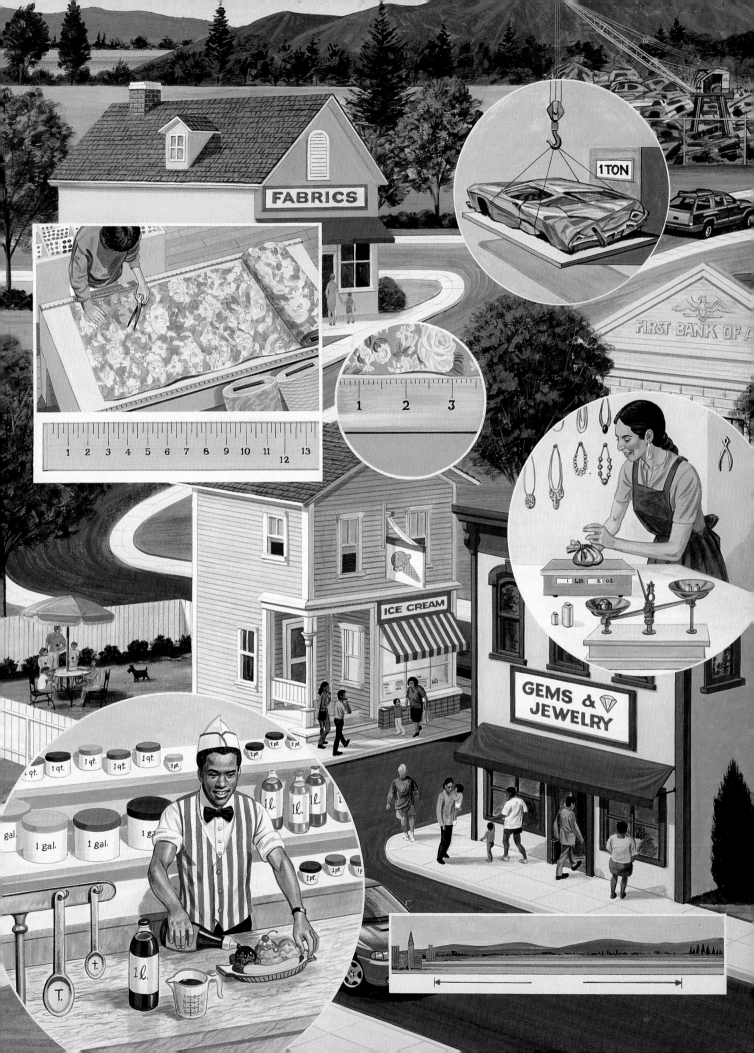

FABRICS

1 TON

FIRST BANK OF A

ICE CREAM

GEMS & JEWELRY

1 2 3 4 5 6 7 8 9 10 11 12 13

1 2 3

1 LB. 2 OZ.

1 qt. 1 qt. 1 qt. 1 qt. 1 qt. 1 pt. 1 pt. 1 pt.

gal. 1 gal. 1 gal. 1 gal.

1 pt. 1 pt. 1 p

1 l. 1 l. 1 l.

T. t.

1 l.

NUMBER PATTERNS, FUNCTIONS, AND RELATIONS

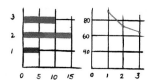 1. graphs

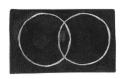 8. random order

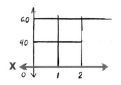 2. x-axis

Ken | 48"
Anna | 56"
Louis | 70"
Zennie | 59"

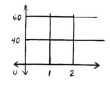 3. y-axis

9. Venn diagram

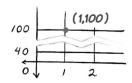 4. coordinates

Student	Height	Weight
Ken	48"	71 lbs
Anna	56"	65 lbs
Louis	70"	100 lbs
Zennie	59"	89 lbs

10. table

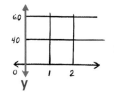 5. coordinate plane

Ken 48" 71 lbs
Anna 56"

 11. chart

 6. ascending order

 12. sequence

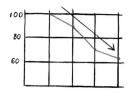 7. descending order

{ 48, 56, 59, 70 } 13. finite set

{ 20, 40, 60, 80... } 14. infinite set

COMPUTERS AND CALCULATORS

 1. personal computer (PC)

 2. monitor

 3. cursor

 4. keyboard

 5. mouse

 6. disk drive

 7. diskette

 8. compact disc (CD)

 9. switch

10. cable

 11. power supply

 12. display

 13. operations keys

 14. equals key

 15. unit key

 16. fraction bar

 17. percent key

 18. clear key

 19. decimal point key

 20. memory recall

NUMBERS

0 zero	13 thirteen	30 thirty
1 one	14 fourteen	40 forty
2 two	15 fifteen	50 fifty
3 three	16 sixteen	60 sixty
4 four	17 seventeen	70 seventy
5 five	18 eighteen	80 eighty
6 six	19 nineteen	90 ninety
7 seven	20 twenty	100 one hundred
8 eight	21 twenty-one	500 five hundred
9 nine	22 twenty-two	
10 ten	23 twenty-three	1,000 one thousand
11 eleven	24 twenty-four	
12 twelve	25 twenty-five	1,000,000 one million

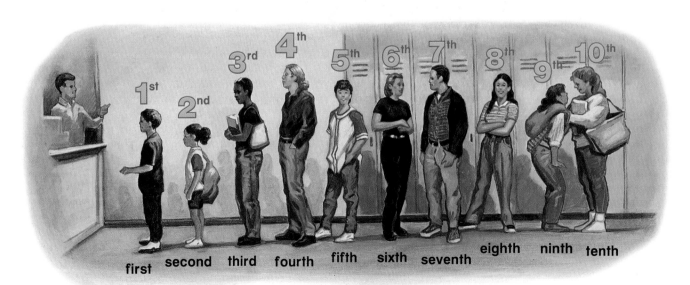

1st first 2nd second 3rd third 4th fourth 5th fifth 6th sixth 7th seventh 8th eighth 9th ninth 10th tenth

TIME

Day

morning

noon

hours   seconds

00:15:30

minutes

afternoon

Night

evening

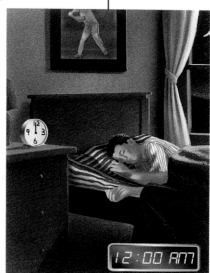

midnight

MONEY

bills

dollar

quarter

nickel

penny

dime

coins

THE CALENDAR

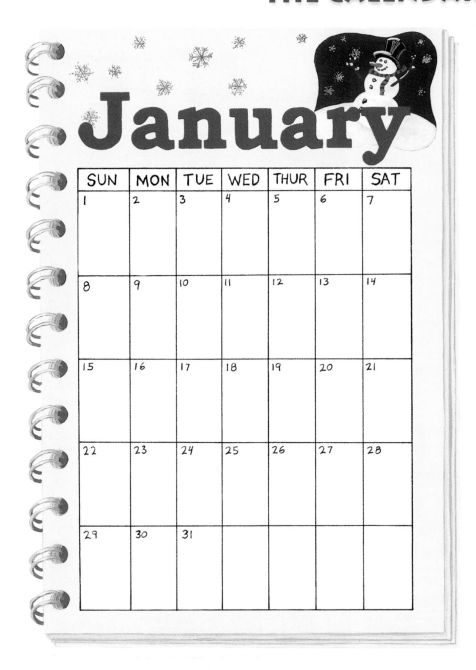

January

SUN	MON	TUE	WED	THUR	FRI	SAT
1	2	3	4	5	6	7
8	9	10	11	12	13	14
15	16	17	18	19	20	21
22	23	24	25	26	27	28
29	30	31				

Months

January	February
March	April
May	June
July	August
September	October
November	December

The Days of the Week

Sunday   Monday   Tuesday   Wednesday   Thursday   Friday   Saturday

COLORS

red   yellow   blue   orange   green   purple

brown   pink   tan   gray   white   black

OPPOSITES

large   small

left   right

tall   short

thick   thin

high   low

empty   full

open   closed

old   new

dirty   clean

FOOD

Breakfast

syrup
eggs
pancakes
bacon
milk
toast
juice
honey
butter
cereal

Lunch

sandwich
pizza
hot dog
mustard
cheese
pudding
salad
soup
cake
ketchup
french fries
hamburger

Dinner

pepper
salt
pie
fruit salad
pasta
mashed potatoes
meat
asparagus

Snacks

peanut butter
popcorn
jelly
yogurt
cookies
bread
peanuts
ice cream

CLOTHING

raincoat

ski cap

scarf

jacket

mittens

baseball cap

sweatshirt

jeans

sneakers

boots

T-shirt

sweater

sweatpants

gloves

dress

ring

blouse

skirt

shorts

underwear

underpants

tights

shoes

earrings

shirt

tie

belt

bracelet

coat

suit

pants

bathrobe

pajamas

slippers

nightgown

socks

WORLD MAP

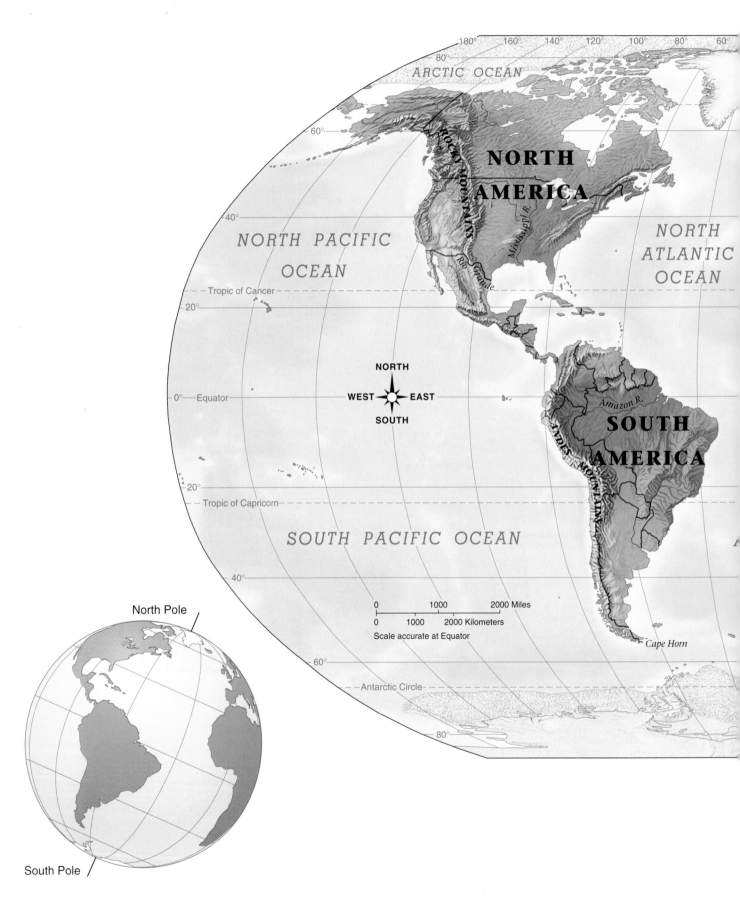

ARCTIC OCEAN

NORTH AMERICA

ROCKY MOUNTAINS

Mississippi R.

Rio Grande

NORTH PACIFIC OCEAN

Tropic of Cancer

NORTH ATLANTIC OCEAN

NORTH
WEST — EAST
SOUTH

Equator

Amazon R.

SOUTH AMERICA

ANDES MOUNTAINS

Tropic of Capricorn

SOUTH PACIFIC OCEAN

| 0 | 1000 | 2000 Miles |
| 0 | 1000 | 2000 Kilometers |

Scale accurate at Equator

Cape Horn

Antarctic Circle

North Pole

South Pole

EUROPE

ASIA

AFRICA

AUSTRALIA

ANTARCTICA

ARCTIC OCEAN

PACIFIC OCEAN

INDIAN OCEAN

Arctic — Circle

ALPS

ATLAS MTS.

URAL MTS.

Volga R.

Ob R.

HIMALAYAS

Yangtze R.

Nile R.

Niger R.

Cape of
Good Hope

20° 40° 60° 80° 100° 120° 140° 160° 180°

80°

60°

40°

20°

0°

20°

0°

60°

80°

IC
N

WORD LIST

The numbers to the right of the entries indicate the page on which the word is introduced. Words in black are the content words found in the illustration. Words in pink appear in a topic's title or can be found as labels or text within a topic's main illustration.

A

abdomen 82
across 52
actor 34
actress 34
acute angle 114
Adams, John 48
add 110
adobe 42
advertisement 22
Africa 128–129
afternoon 123
agriculture 26
air pollution 96
airplane 14
Alabama 20
Alaska 20
Alaska Pipeline 30
alligator 86
allosaurus 94
ambulance 16
American Samoa 20
ammunition 54
amoeba 78
amphibians 86
anatosaurus 94
angles 114
angry 66
animals 70
ankle 60
ankylosaurus 94
ant 82
Antarctica 128–129
antennae 80
Anthony, Susan B. 58
apartment building 10
apatosaurus 94
apple 76
Appomattox 55
apprentice 44
April 124
arachnids 82

B

arch 42
Arctic Ocean 128–129
area 114
Arizona 20
Arkansas 20
arm 60
around 52
arrow 38
artery 62
ascending order 118
Asia 128–129
asparagus 126
assembly line 24
Atlantic Ocean 128–129
atmosphere 108
atom 98
attic 6
auditorium 4
August 124
aunt 8
Australia 128–129
avocado 76
axle 100

baby 8
bacon 126
ballot 56
banana 76
bandage 16
bank 10
bark 72
barn 14
barnacles 80
barrel 50
Barton, Clara 58
base 114
baseball cap 127
basement 6
basket 38
basketball 12
bass 84

bat 92
bathrobe 127
bathroom 6
bathtub 6
battle 46
bay 44
bayonet 46
beak 88
bear 92
beautiful 33
bed 16
bedroom 6
bee 82
bell 42
Bell, Alexander Graham 58
belt 127
bicycle 12
Bill of Rights 56
bills 123
birds 88
black 124
blacksmith 44
blanket 16
blizzard 108
block 12
blood vessels 62
blouse 127
blue 124
bluefish 84
boat 30
body 60
boil 98
bone 62
book 2
boots 127
born 48
both 119
bottle 96
bow 38
boys room 4
bracelet 127
brachiosaurus 94
brain 62

branch 72
bread 126
breakfast 126
bridge 14
bright 64
broccoli 74
brother 8
brown 124
bud 72
buffalo 28
bulb 72
Bull Run 55
bulletin board 2
bunny 90
bus 10
businessperson 22
butter 126
butterfly 82
buy 22

C

cabbage 74
cabin 50
cable 120
cactus 32
cafeteria 4
cake 126
calculators 120
calendar 124
calf 90
California 20
camel 92
camera 34
campsite 50
Canada 36
canal 50
candidate 56
candles 42
cannery 30
cannon 46
cannonball 46
canoe 50
can 96
cantaloupe 76
canteen 54
cape 44
capital 36
car 12
cardinal 88

cargo 40
carnivores 95
carpenter 18
carpool 96
carrot 74
cartilage 62
cartoon 48
cassette player 2
cast 16
cat 90
caterpillar 82
catfish 84
cattle 26
cauliflower 74
ceiling 6
celery 74
cell membrane 70
cell wall 70
cells 70
cemetery 54
centimeter 116
cereal 126
ceremony 38
chain saw 30
chair 2
chalkboard 2
chameleon 86
chart (n.) 68
chart (v.) 118
Chavez, Cesar 58
cheese 126
chemical change 98
cherry 76
chest 60
chicken 88
chicken coop 14
chief 38
chimney 6
chin 60
choices 119
chromosome 70
chrysalis 82
church 10
circle 112
circumference 114
citizens 56
citrus 76
city 10
Civil War, The 54
clam 80

classify 69
classroom 2
claw 80
clean 125
clear key 120
cliff dwelling 38
climates 106
clipper ship 52
closed 125
closet 6
cloth 24
clothing 127
cloud 108
coach 4
coat 127
cobra 86
cockroach 82
cod 84
coins 123
cold 66
collection 68
colonial life 44
Colorado 20
colors 124
Columbus, Christopher 40
combine 26
comet 102
common 44
communication 22
compact disc (CD) 120
comparisons 110
compass 114
compass rose 36
compost 96
compound 98
computer 2
computer operator 18
computers 120
conch 80
cone 112
Confederacy 54
Congress 56
congruent figures 114
Connecticut 20
constellation 102
Constitution 56
construction worker 18
Continental Divide 28
Continental soldier 46
cookies 126

O

P

teach 42
teacher 2
teaspoon 116
technology 34
teeth 60
telephone 22
television 22
temperate forest 106
temperate zones 106
temperature 108
temple 10
ten 122
tendon 62
Tennessee 20
tent 52
tentacles 80
tenth 122
tepee 38
territories 21
Texas 20
Thanksgiving 44
thermometer 16
thick 125
thin 125
third 122
thirsty 66
thirteen 122
thirty 122
thorax 82
thread 24
three 122
thumb 60
Thursday 124
tick 82
tie 127
tiger 92
tights 127
timber 30
time 123
tired 66
toad 86
toast 126
tobacco 44
toe 60
toilet 6
tomahawk 46
tomato 76
ton 116
tornado 108
totem pole 36

touch 64
tourism 34
tourist 34
town meeting 44
tractor 14
trading post 42
traffic light 10
trail 50
train 14
trapper 50
tree 72
triangle 112
tribe 38
triceratops 94
tropical zone 106
trout 84
truck 14
trunk 72
Tubman, Harriet 58
Tucson 43
Tuesday 124
tuna 84
tundra 106
turkey 88
turtle 86
tusk 92
tweezers 68
twelve 122
twenty 122
twenty-five 122
twenty-four 122
twenty-one 122
twenty-three 122
twenty-two 122
two 122
tyrannosaurus 94

U

U.S. Virgin Islands 20
uncle 8
underpants 127
underwear 127
uniform 54
Union 54
unit key 120
United States 20
universe 102
Uranus 102
Utah 20

V

valley 104
van 12
vegetables 74
vein 62
Venn diagram 118
Venus 102
Vermont 20
vertebrates 70
vest 127
Vikings 40
vines 106
Virginia 20
volcano 104
vote 56

W

wagon 14
wagon train 50
wall 6
wampum 38
Washington 20
Washington, George 58
wastebasket 2
water fountain 4
water pollution 96
water storage 32
watermelon 76
wave 40
weather 108
weave 38
web 82
webbed foot 86
wedge 100
Wednesday 124
weight 116
welcome 3
well 32
west 128-129
West, The 28
West Coast 34
West Virginia 20
wetland 104
whale 92
wheat 26
wheel 100
wheelchair 16
white 124